Songs and Cries of London Town

Bob Chilcott

a 'capital' choral cantata for SATB choir, upper-voice choir, piano duet, and optional percussion

MUSIC DEPARTMENT

OXFORD
UNIVERSITY PRESS

Great Clarendon Street, Oxford OX2 6DP, England
198 Madison Avenue, New York, NY10016, USA

Oxford University Press is a department of the University of Oxford.
It furthers the University's aim of excellence in research, scholarship,
and education by publishing worldwide in

Oxford New York
Auckland Bangkok Buenos Aires Cape Town Chennai
Dar es Salaam Delhi Hong Kong Istanbul Karachi Kolkata
Kuala Lumpur Madrid Melbourne Mexico City Mumbai Nairobi
São Paulo Shanghai Taipei Tokyo Toronto

First published 2001

ISBN 978-0-19-343297-0

Printed in Great Britain on acid-free paper by
Halstan & Co. Ltd., Amersham, Bucks.

London bells (No. 3), with accompaniment arranged for one piano,
is also available as a stand-alone piece in a separate leaflet
alongside the upper-voice part for *Good morrow!* (No. 5).
The leaflet (BC47a, ISBN 0-19-343333-8) may be used in
conjunction with this vocal score.

Commissioned by and dedicated to Colin Durrant and the Barnet Choral Society, on the occasion of the choir's Diamond Jubilee

Songs and Cries of London Town

1. *Come buy*

Anon (17th century)

BOB CHILCOTT

Printed in Great Britain

OXFORD UNIVERSITY PRESS, MUSIC DEPARTMENT, GREAT CLARENDON STREET, OXFORD OX2 6DP

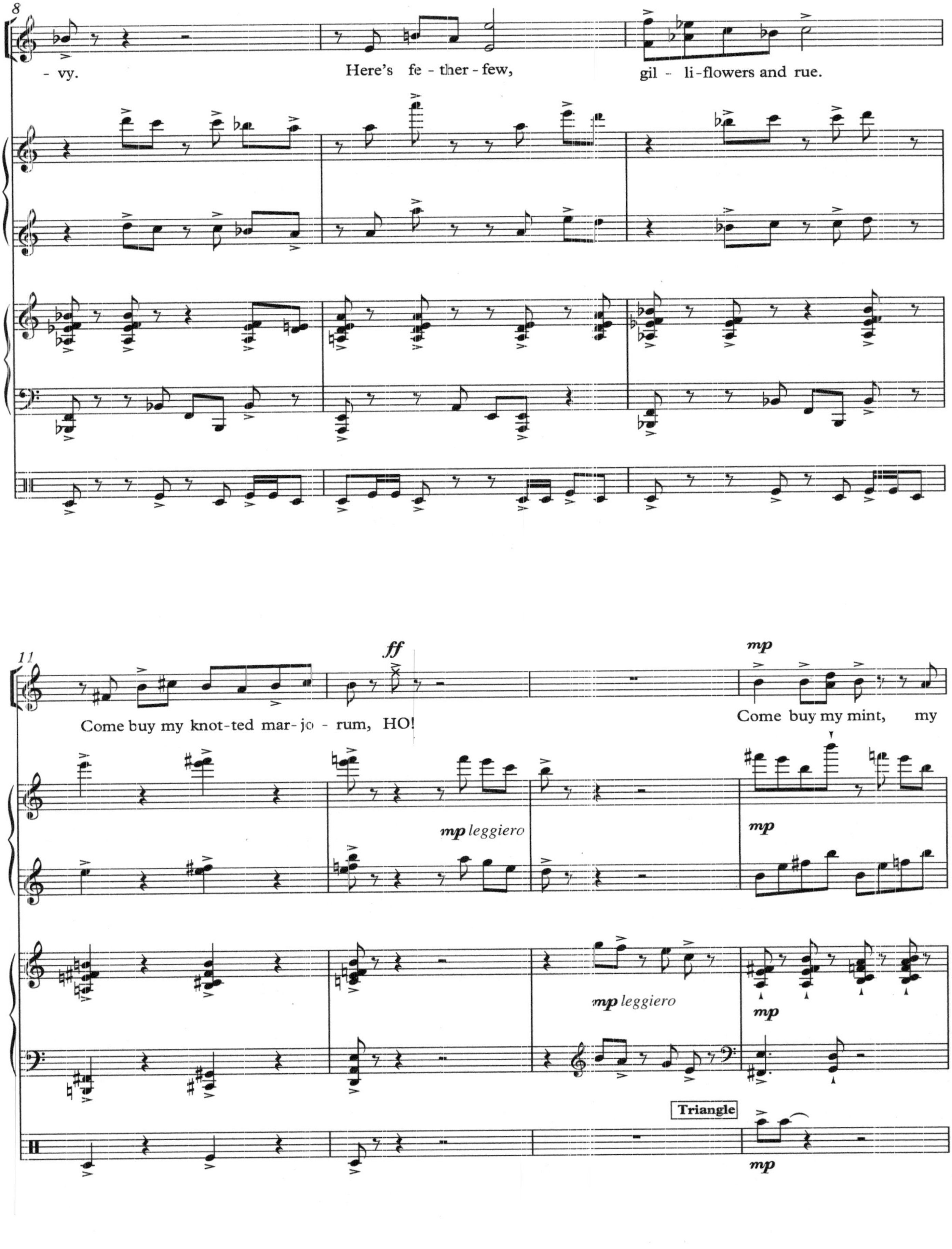

11

ff

mp

Come buy my knot - ted mar - jo - rum, HO!

Come buy my mint, my

mp leggiero

mp

mp leggiero

mp

Triangle

mp

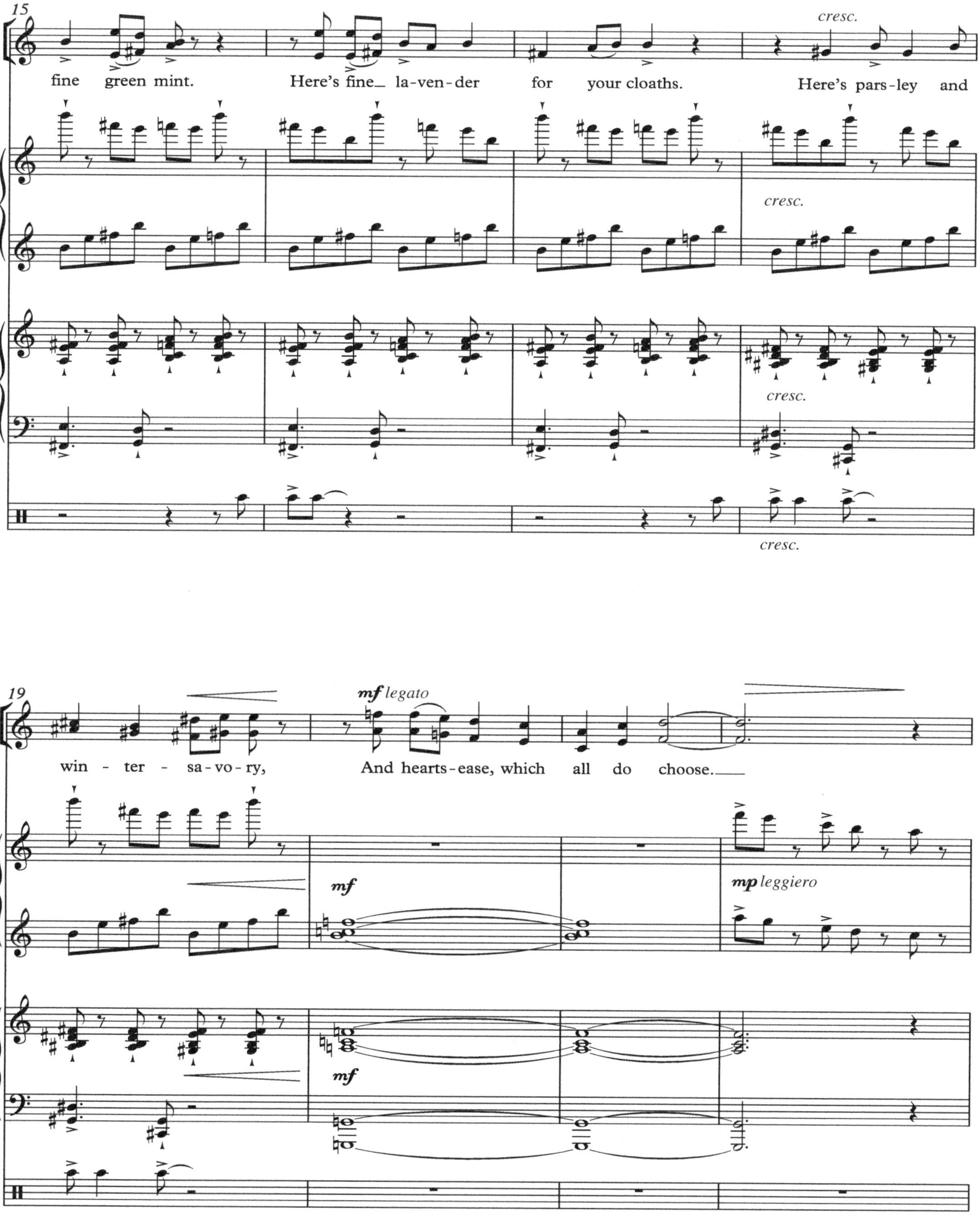

15

cresc.

fine green mint. Here's fine_ la-ven-der for your cloaths. Here's pars-ley and

cresc.

cresc.

cresc.

23
mp
mf cresc.
Here's balm and his-sop, and cinque - foil,
All fine herbs, it is well known.
mp
mf
mp
mf
mp
27
f
Let none des-pise the mer - ry, mer-ry cries of
TENORS & BASSES f
Let none des - pise the mer - ry, mer - ry
f
f
Bongos
mf
f

30
gliss.
f
fa - mous Lon - don town!
Let none des-pise the
gliss.
cries of fa - mous Lon - don town!
Let none des -
33
ff
mer - ry, mer - ry cries of fa - mous Lon - don town! HO!
-pise the mer - ry cries of fa - mous Lon - don town! HO!
ff
f
ff
f
ff
f

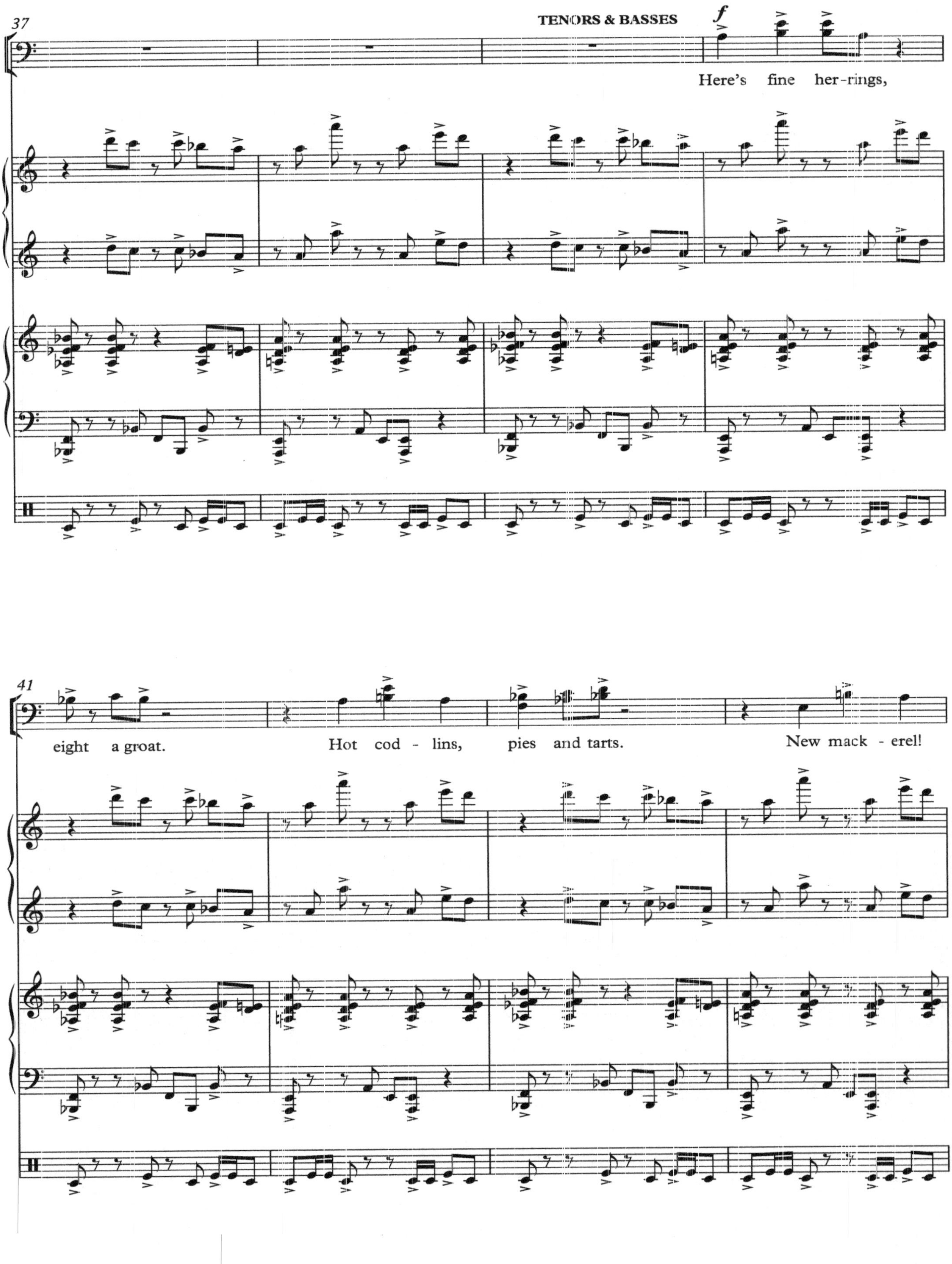

41

eight a groat. Hot cod - lins, pies and tarts. New mack - erel!

45

ff

have to sell. Come buy my Well - fleet oys - ters, HO!

mp leggiero

mp leggiero

mp

49

cresc.

Come buy my whit - ings fine and new. Wives, shall I mend your hus - bands' horns? I'll

mp

mp

Triangle

mp

53
mf espress.
grind your knives to please your wives, And ve - ry nice - ly cut your
cresc.
mf
cresc.
mf
cresc.
57
mp
mf cresc.
corns. Maids, have you a - ny hair to sell, Ei - ther flax - en,
mp leggiero
mp
mf
mp
mf
mp

SOPRANOS & ALTOS
Let none des-pise the mer-ry, mer-ry cries of
black or brown?
Let none des - pise the mer-ry, mer-ry
Bongos
fa - mous Lon-don town!
gliss.
Let none des-pise the mer-ry, mer-ry cries of
cries of fa - mous Lon-don town!
Let none des - pise the mer-ry cries of

69
ff
fa - mous Lon - don town! HO!
ff
fa - mous Lon - don town! HO!
ff
f
ff
f
ff
f
73
f
Here's fine_ ros-ma - ry, sage, and_ thyme.
f
Here's fine her-rings, eight a groat.

77
Come buy my ground i - vy.
Here's fe-ther-few,
Hot cod - lins, pies and tarts.
New mack - erel!
80
gil - li-flowers and rue.
Come buy my knot-ted mar-jo - rum, HO!
ff
have to sell.
Come buy my Well - fleet oys - ters, HO!
ff
mp leggiero

83
mp
Come buy my mint, my fine green_ mint. Here's fine_ la-ven-der
mp
Come buy my whit - ings fine and new. Wives, shall I mend your
mp
mp leggiero
mp
Triangle
mp
87
cresc.
for your_ cloaths. Here's pars-ley and win - ter - sa-vo-ry, And hearts - ease, which
mf legato
cresc.
hus - bands' horns? I'll grind your knives to please your wives,_ And ve - ry
mf espress.
cresc.
mf
cresc.
mf
cresc.

91
mp
mf cresc.
all do choose.
Here's balm and his - sop, and cinque - foil,
All fine herbs, it
mp
mf cresc.
nice - ly cut your corns.
Maids, have you a - ny hair to sell,
Ei - ther flax - en,
mp leggiero
mp
mf
mp
mf
mp
96
f
is well known.
Let none des - pise the mer - ry, mer - ry cries of
f
black or brown?
Let none des - pise the mer - ry, mer - ry
f
f
Bongos
mf
f

100
gliss.
f
fa - mous Lon - don
town!
Let none des - pise
the
mer - ry, mer - ry cries
of
gliss.
f
cries
of fa - mous
Lon - don
town!
Let none des - pise
the mer - ry cries of
104
ff
fa - mous Lon - don
town!
Let none des - pise
the
mer - ry, mer - ry cries
of
ff
fa - mous Lon - don
town!
ff
ff
f
ff

108
fa - mous Lon - don town!
gliss.
ff
Let none des-pise the
111
mer-ry, mer-ry cries Of fa - mous Lon - don town! HO!
fff
attacca

2. *The flower of Cities all*

William Dunbar (1465?–1530?)

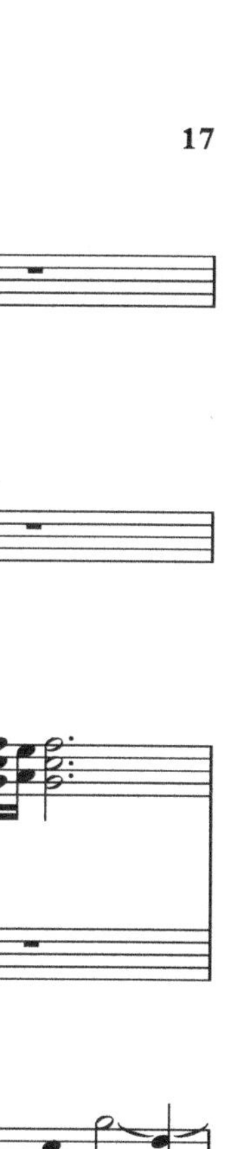

123
poco rit.
a tempo
dolce
p
wal - lès run-neth down;
dolce
p
poco rit.
a tempo
p
p sost.
6
p dolce
128
SOPRANOS
p legato
Where many a swan doth swim with
6
3
p legato
p

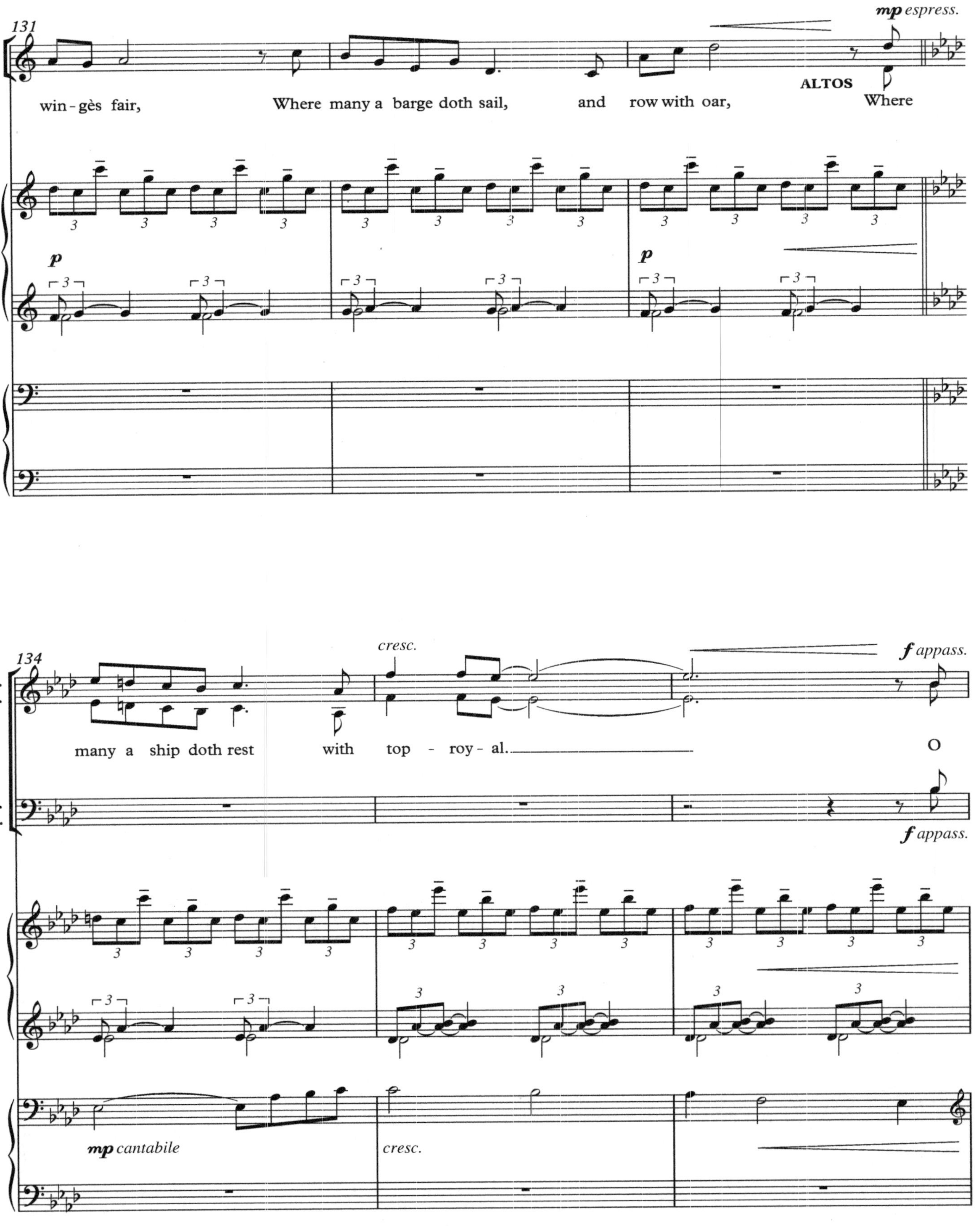

134
f appass.
cresc.
S.
A.
many a ship doth rest
with
top - roy - al.
O
T.
B.
f appass.
mp cantabile
cresc.

137
town of town - ès, pa - tron and not com - pare,
f
Large suspended cymbal
tr
mf
ff molto dim.
140
Lon - don,
ff molto dim.
ff molto dim.
p dolce
ff molto dim.
mp
p
ff

143
poco rit.
a tempo
p dolce
mp espress.
S.
thou_ art
the flower of Ci - - ties all,
A.
thou_ art the flower of Ci - ties all, of Ci - ties all, the
T.
thou_ art the flower, the flower of
B.
thou_ art the flower of_ Ci - - ties all,
146
p
pp
the flower of Ci - ties all, the flower of
flower of Ci - ties all, of Ci - ties all, the flower of Ci - ties all, of
Ci - ties all, the flower, the flower of Ci - ties all, of
the flower of_ Ci - ties all, the flower of_

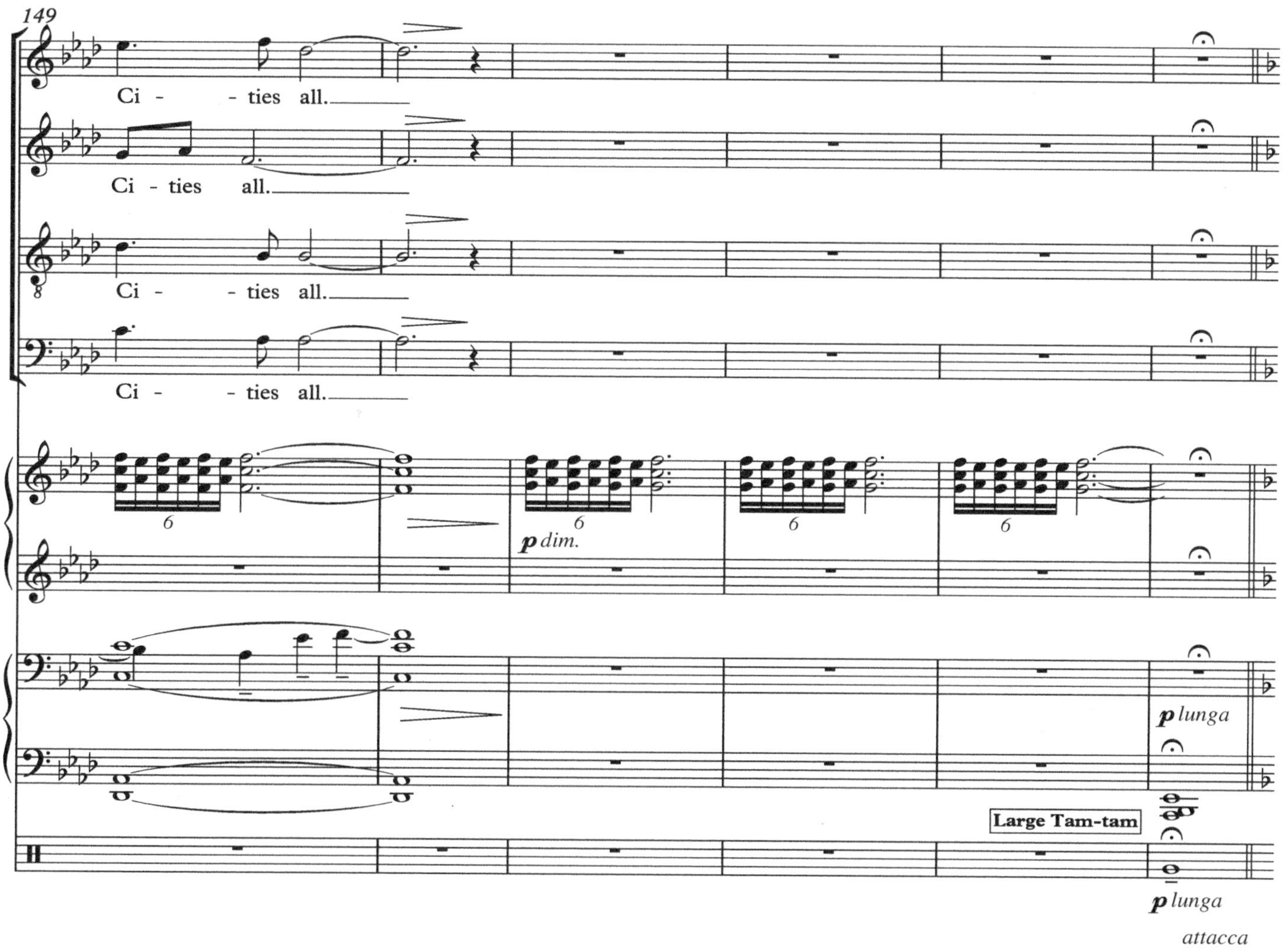

149
Ci - ties all.
Ci - ties all.
Ci - ties all.
Ci - ties all.
6
6
p dim.
6
6
p lunga
Large Tam-tam
p lunga
attacca

3. *London bells*

Anon. (early 18th century)

155
On time! ♩=c.162
UPPER-VOICE CHOIR mf
Two sticks and an ap -
mf leggiero
Tubular Bells
mf

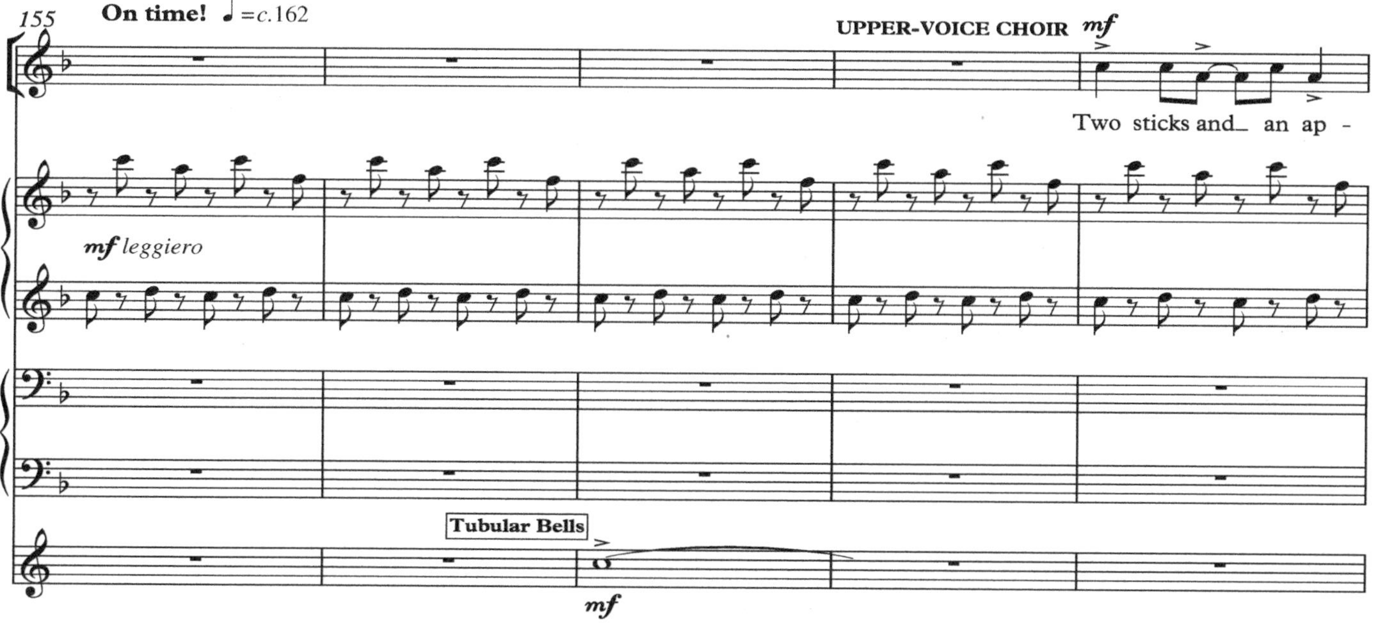

160
-ple,
Ring the bells at White - cha - pel.

165
Old Fa - ther Bald Pate,
Ring the bells Ald - gate.

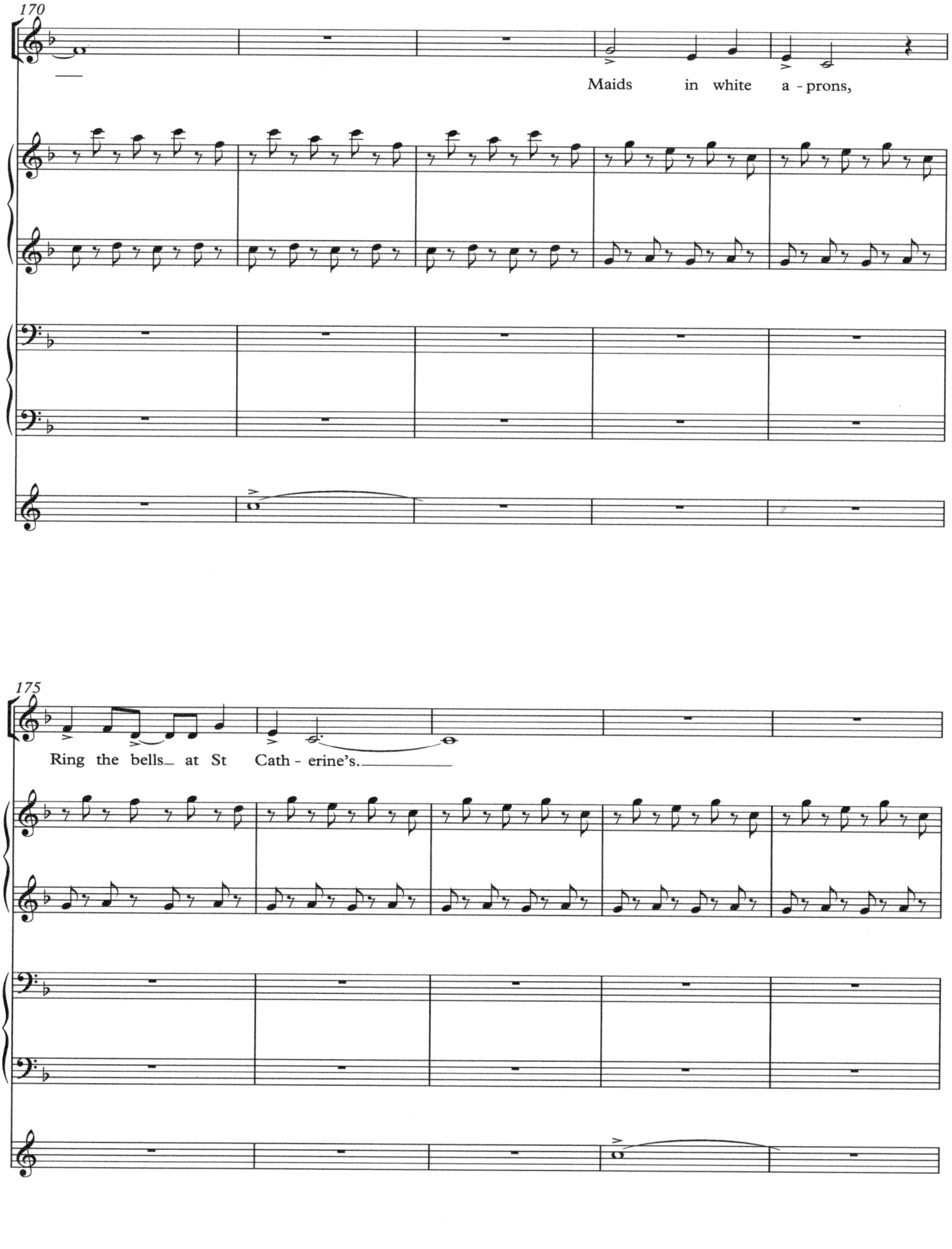

170

Maids in white a - prons,

180
O - ran - ges and le - mons,
Ring the bells at St Cle - ment's.

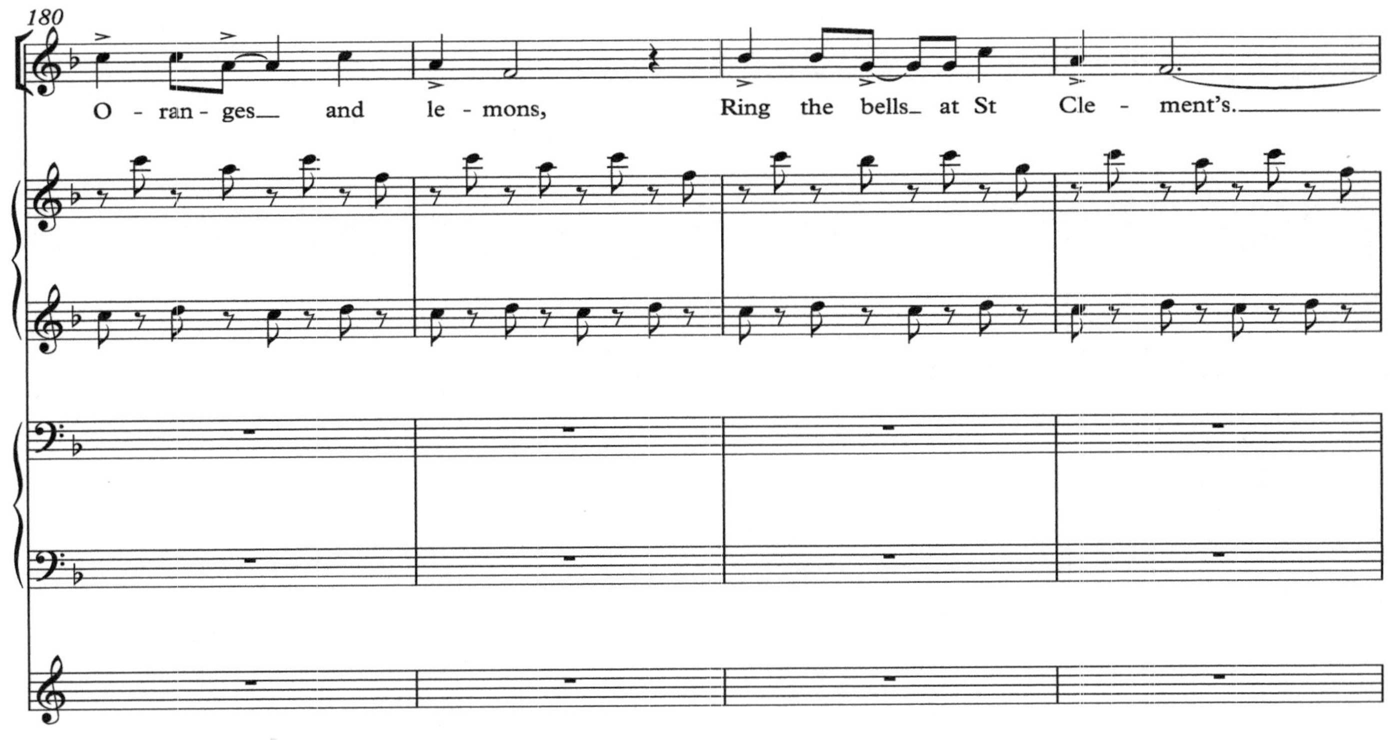

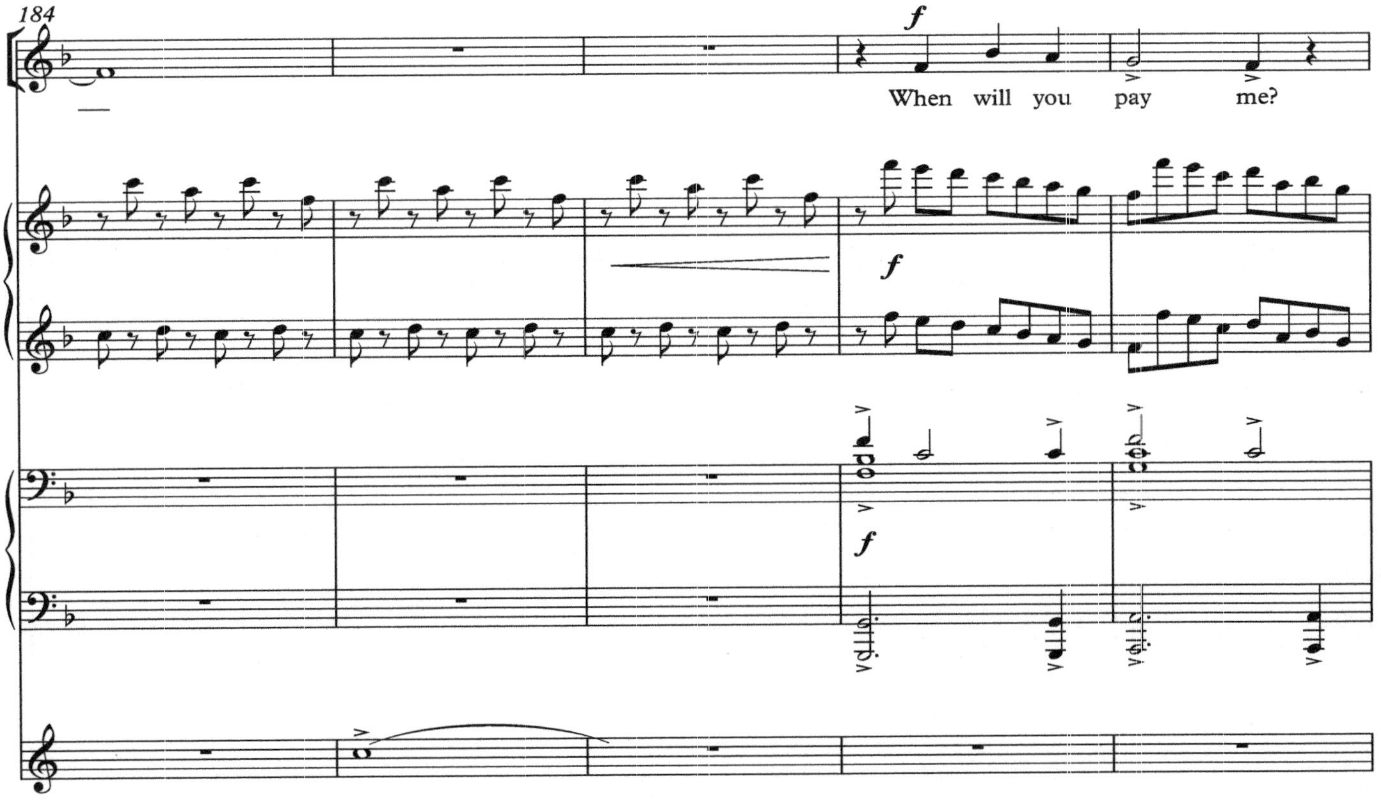
184
f
When will you pay me?
f
f

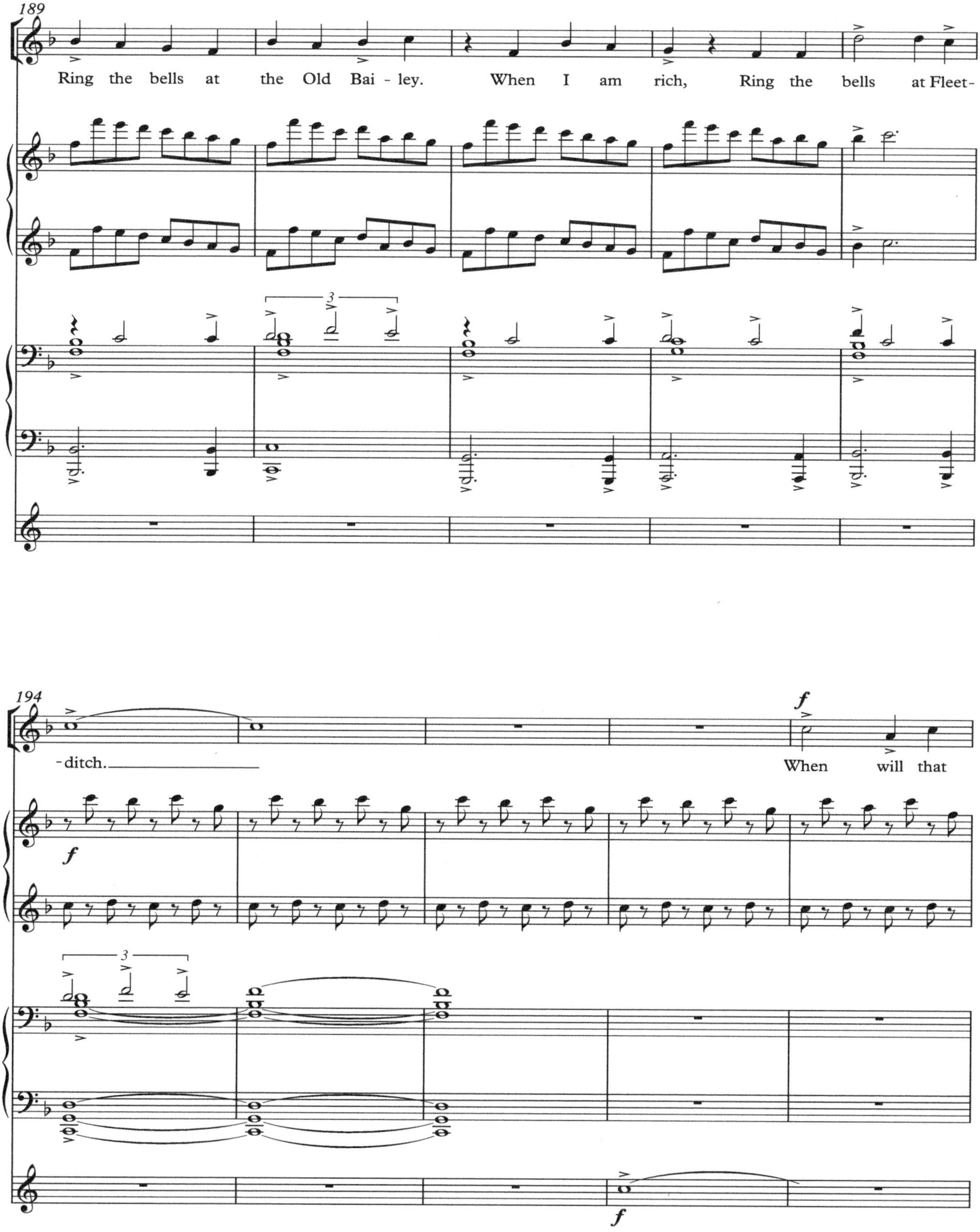

189

Ring the bells at the Old Bai - ley. When I am rich, Ring the bells at Fleet-

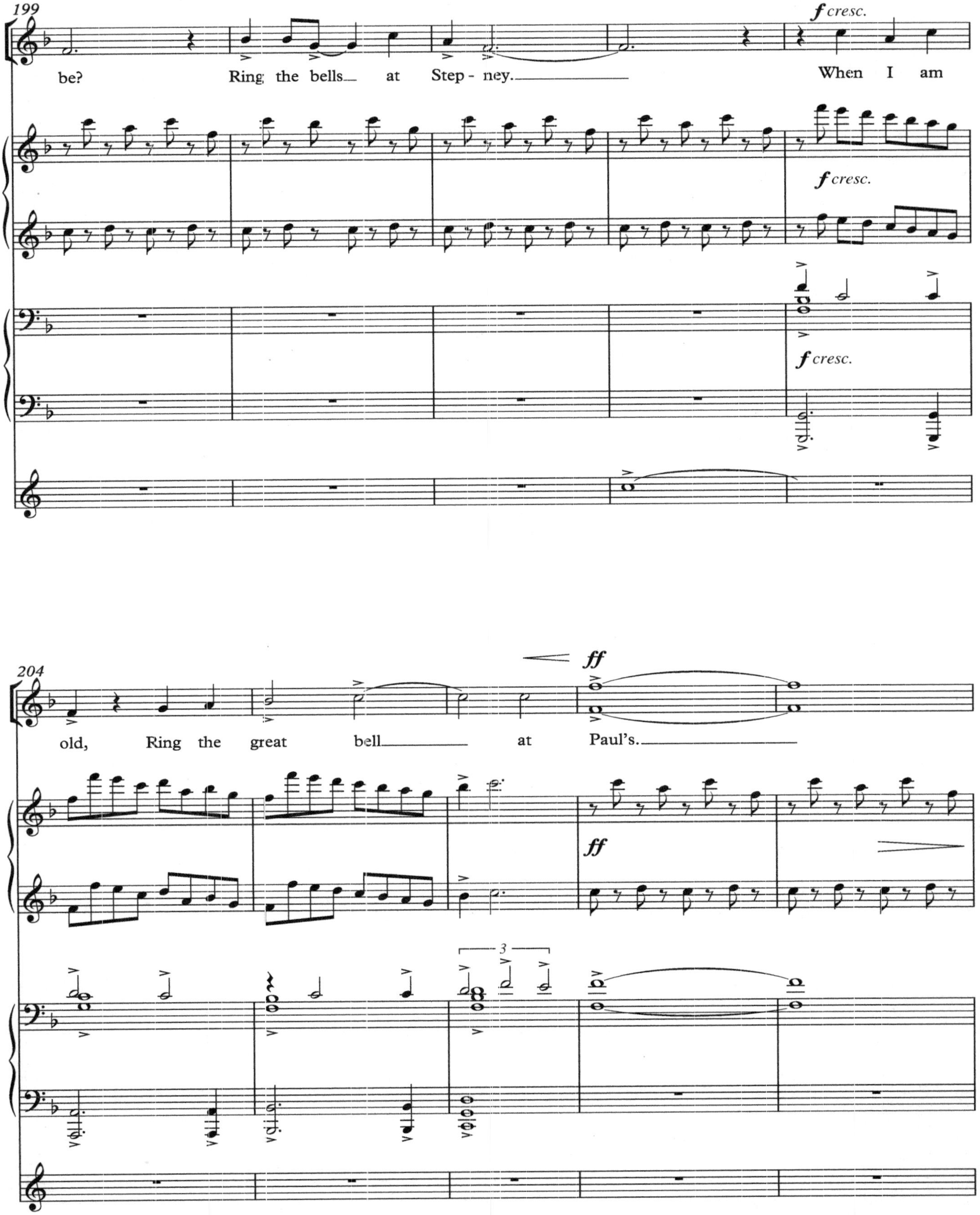

204

ff

old, Ring the great bell at Paul's.

ff

3

209

f

Two sticks and an ap - ple,

f

f

mf

213

Ring the bells at White - cha - pel.

218
Old Fa - ther Bald Pate, Ring the bells_ Ald - gate.

222
Maids in white a - prons,
mf

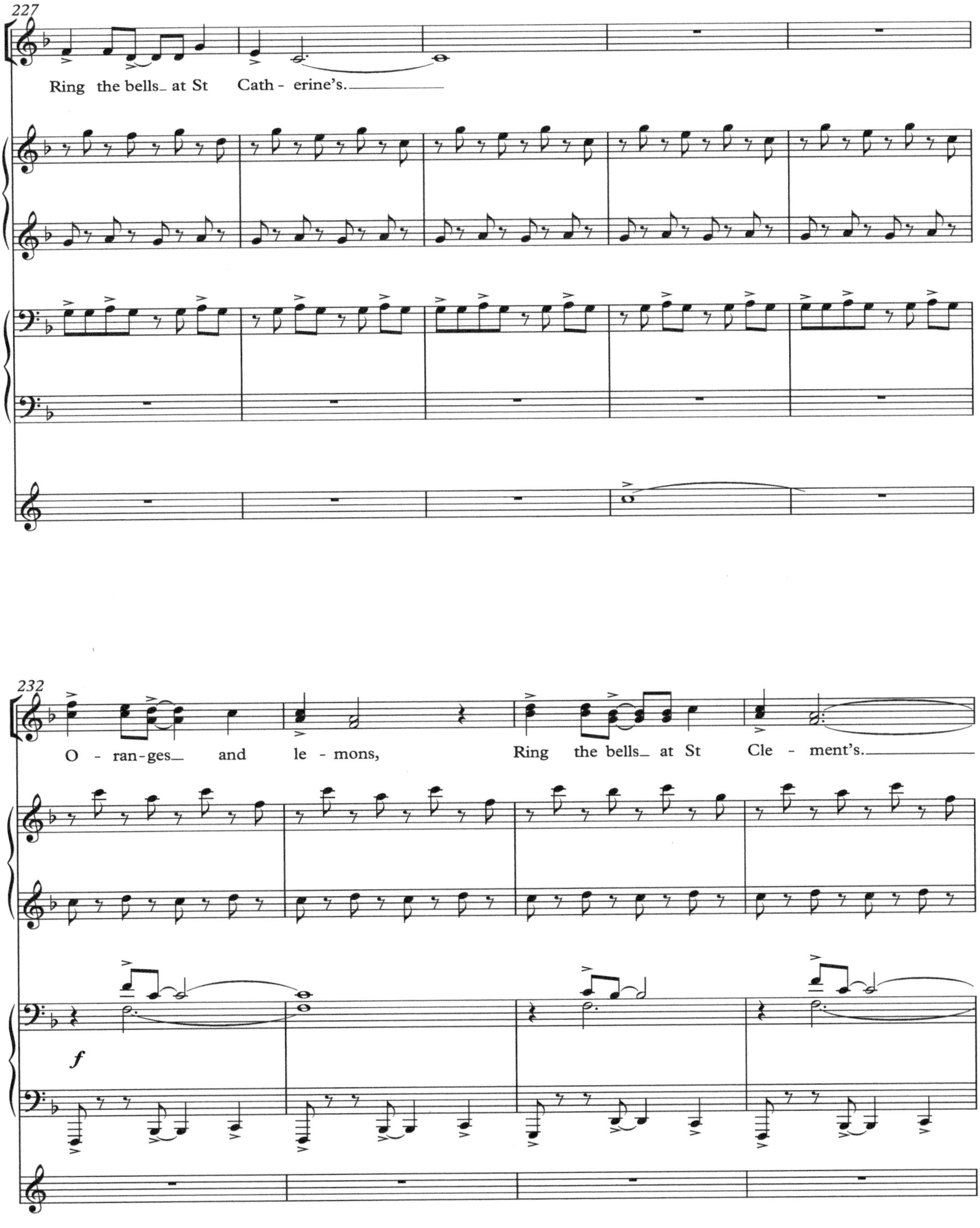

227

Ring the bells at St Cath - erine's.

236

f

When will you pay me?

f

f

f

3

3

241

Ring the bells at the Old Bai - ley. When I am rich, Ring the bells at Fleet-

3

3

3

3

3

246
f
- ditch.
When will that
f
3
3
3
251
be?
Ring the bells at Step - ney.
f

255
f cresc.
When I am old, Ring the great bell at
f cresc.
f cresc.
259
ff
Paul's.
ff
dim.
ff
ff
mf

4. *Composed upon Westminster Bridge, September 3, 1802*

William Wordsworth (1770–1850)

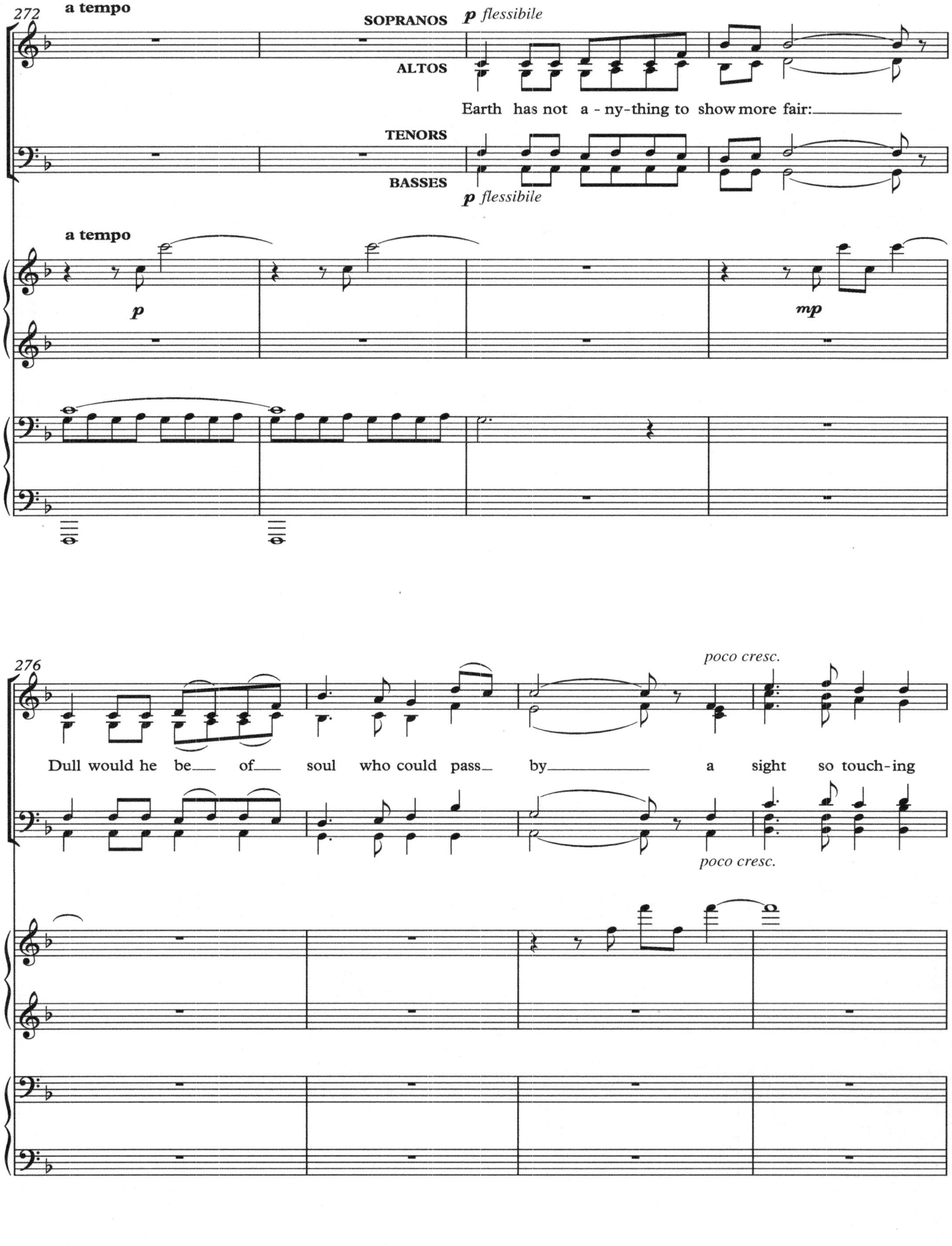

272 **a tempo**

SOPRANOS ***p*** *flessibile*

ALTOS

Earth has not a - ny-thing to show more fair:

TENORS

BASSES ***p*** *flessibile*

a tempo

p

mp

280

p This City now doth like a

in its ma-jes-ty: This Ci-ty now doth like a gar-ment wear the

p

mp

mp

284

beau-ty of the morn-ing;

p

Si - lent,

p

mp espress.

p

p

289
mp cresc.
bare,
Ships,
to-wers,
domes,
the - a - tres and tem-ples lie
mp cresc.
mp cresc.
293
f
mp dolce e dim.
o - pen un-to the fields and to the sky;
All bright and glit-ter-ing
mp dolce e dim.
f
All bright and
f
mp dolce
f

poco rit. a tempo

p espress.

297

— in the smoke - less air. — Ne - ver did sun more

glit - ter - ing in the smoke - less air. —

poco rit. a tempo

mp

p espress.

mp dolce

p espress.

301

beau - ti - ful - ly steep in his first splen - dour val - ley, rock, or hill;

304
poco rit.
p dolce
Ne'er_ saw I, ne-ver felt, a calm so deep!
poco rit.
dolce
dolce
308 a tempo
poco rit.
a tempo
poco rit.
p semplice
p semplice

313
a tempo
p
The ri - ver gli-deth at his own sweet will; Dear
p
a tempo
p
mp
317
poco rit.
a little slower
God! the ve - ry hous - es seem a - sleep; and all that migh-ty
poco rit.
a little slower
mp dolce
mp dolce

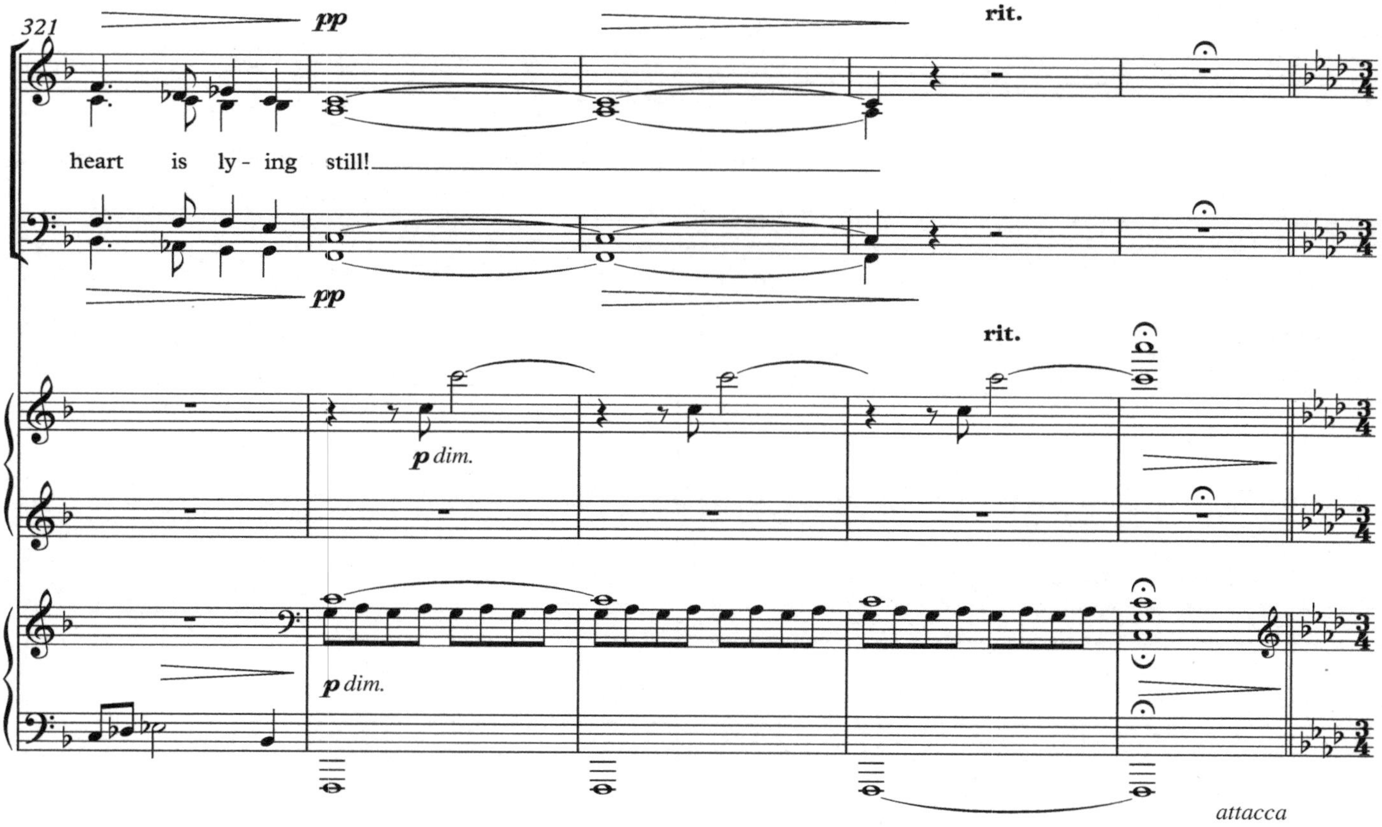

321 pp rit.

heart is ly - ing still!

pp

rit.

p dim.

p dim.

attacca

5. *Good morrow!*

Anon. (17th century, adapted)

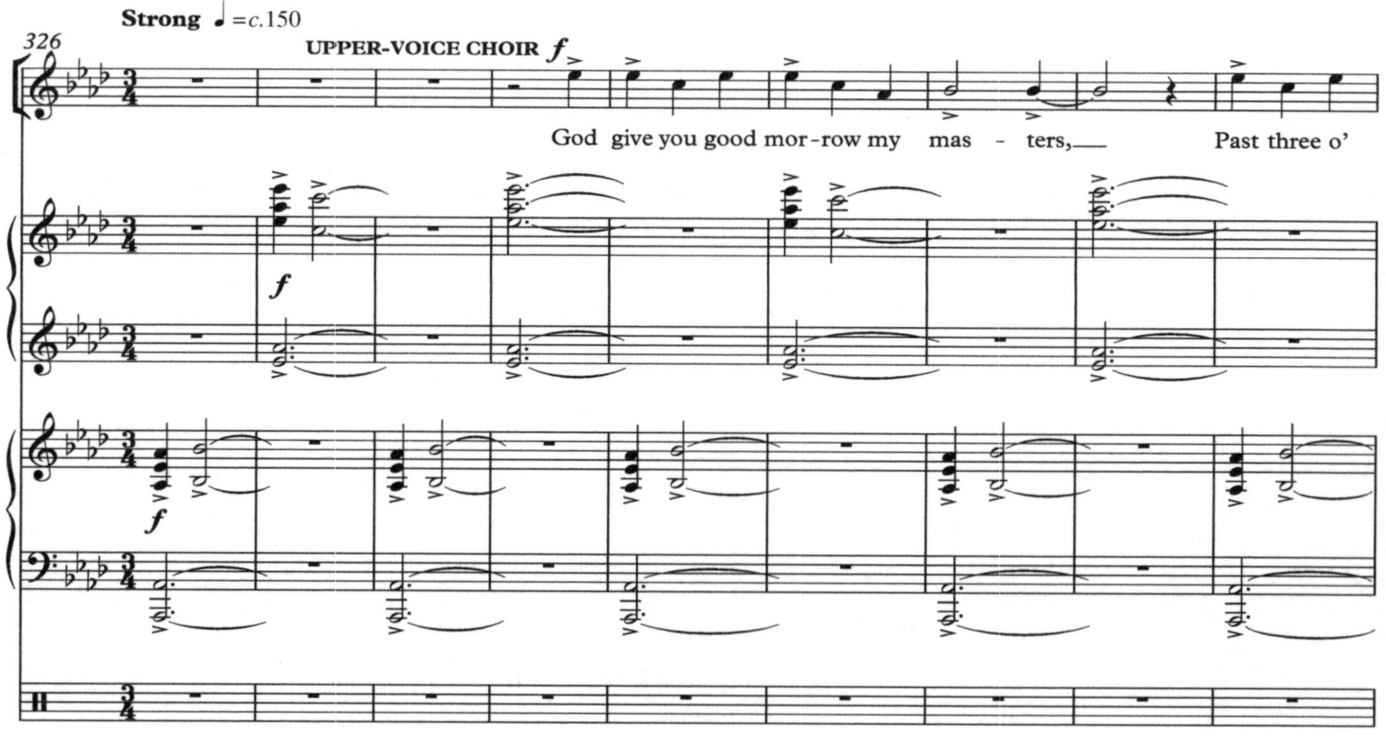

335
clock and a fair mor - ning.
p
p

TENORS & BASSES unis.
343
f
A good saus-age, a good, and it be roast - ed.

SOPRANOS & ALTOS unis.
348
f
Go round a-bout the ca - pon, go round.
f
Hot cod - lings,
cresc.
cresc.
353
New oys - ters, new!
mf
Young cab-bage
hot!
mf
White cab-bage, white,
p sub.
p sub.

357
UPPER-VOICE CHOIR
Broom,
white,
Young par-snips,
white, HEY!
White tur-nips, white,
HEY!
cresc.
cresc.
Tambourine
364
broom,
broom!

371
SOPRANOS & ALTOS unis.
Will ye buy a
TENORS & BASSES unis.
Have you a-ny work for a tink-er?
376
mat for a bed?
New thorn-backs,
New had-dock, new!
cresc.
cresc.

382
new!
Ripe goose-ber-ries ripe,
Ripe peas-cods,
Ripe chest-nuts, ripe,
Ripe small nuts, ripe,
p sub.
cresc.
p sub.
cresc.
tr
mf
385
ff
ripe, HEY!
ff
HEY!
Sweep, chim-ney sweep,
mis - tress,
TENORS f
BASSES f Sweep, chim - ney sweep,
ff
mf
ff
mf
ff

391

f

With a hey der-ry, der-ry, der-ry sweep.

mis - tress,

f

TENORS & BASSES *unis.*

From the

396

Sweep, chim - ney, sweep,

cresc.

bot - tom to the top, sweep, chim - ney sweep, Then shall no

cresc.

401
Your por - ridge pot, With a
soot fall in your por - ridge pot, With a hey der - ry, der - ry,
mf cresc.
f
405
ff
hey der - ry, der - ry, der - ry sweep!
der - ry sweep, der - ry der - ry sweep!
f

409

UPPER-VOICE CHOIR *f*

Ripe straw - ber-ries, ripe!

f

416

CH.

BASSES *f*

Have you a - ny

p

cresc.

p

cresc.

421
f
Cher - ry ripe,
ap - ples fine,
Cher - ry ripe,
Will you buy my dish of
Fresh cheese and cream,
Ripe goose - ber-ries, ripe,
work for a coop - er?

426
ap - ples fine,
eels?
Fine Se - ville
Hot ap - ple pies, hot, hot pip - pen pies, hot, Fine
Buy an - y ink, will you buy an - y peas?
Hard on - ions, hard,
cresc.
cresc.

430
ff
Have you
o - - ran - ges,
Young cab - bage,
le - mons,
le - mons,
Young cab - bage,
Hard gar - lic, hard,
White cab - bage, white,
Ripe dam - - sons,
White cab - bage, white,

433
f
a - ny old bel - lows or trays to mend? We make an
white, Young tur-nips, white, Young par-snips, white. We make an
white, Young tur-nips, white, Young par-snips, white. We make an
White tur-nips, white, White par-snips, white. We make an
White tur-nips, white, White par-snips, white. We make an

436
ff
end.
fff
HEY!
ff
end.
fff
HEY!
ff
end.
fff
HEY!
ff
end.
fff
HEY!
ff
end.
fff
HEY!
ff
fff
ff
fff
tr
ff
fff